MAGICAL
TRAINS/STRANGE
FIRE

A COLLECTION OF OLD
AND NEW POEMS

GABRIEL EMANUEL

For Avia and Shiloh
May you follow your dreams
wherever they take you
and never let go

CONTENTS

Strange Fire

AS FLIES PURIFY THE AIR

As flies purify

the air

brushing dirty little wings and legs

everywhere

So do poems cleanse

the empty page

raining Hell bent letters

on some future age

I REFUSE TO DONATE MY ORGANS TO SCIENCE

I refuse to donate my organs to science
nor my ribs to Western architects
when the next to last woman comes to claim
a refund on my heart
say it is with the first
who stole it.

Cover my expression with a mask
sail my body out to sea
raise up a flag of my favourite shirt
then burn it.

I'm going home.

WHAT IS IT ABOUT MY LUCK?

What is it about my luck

that it always seems the wrong month

for a cowboy to saddle up?

    if I took up the tuba my lungs would collapse

    If I was a builder of bridges the rivers would dry

    If I skydived from Heaven my chute would get stuck

yet I would probably survive

crippled with luck

FIRST LETTER TO COLUMBUS FROM NEW YORK CITY, JUNE, 1980

Give me a ship and a hundred men

it is time to prove the world is round again

I am relating to Columbus

though I hesitate to discover a nation

    of new consumers

I fear I would fall off the edge

if there were nuclear crossbreeds everywhere

and no Indians

IT HAS BEEN A LONG SEASON

It has been a long season

without any rain

come to me slowly

    like a prophet

returning from the wilderness.

Tonight

without clouds

breathless under a liquid mantle of

    hot personal stars

let the beads form like nectar

upon our famished thighs

let the dreams turns to dew drops

    softer

than the animal prayer of our velvet loins.

IN THE SONG OF SONGS

In the Song of Songs
thy two breasts are like two fawns
that are twins of a gazelle
and the Rabbis
stroking their grey beards
pronounced one breast Israel
and her sister the Talmud

Now Solomon when you vowed
you would climb up the palm tree
to take hold of the branches
when you tasted honey and milk under the tongue
moving gently the lips that were a ribbon of scarlet
was it the Talmud that so ravished your heart
was it Israel that burned in your soul?

Oh get to the mountains wise King among lovers
climb up the cliffs where she waits on her bed
lay down your gifts of sex and of wisdom
uncover lost breasts from our beards

STRAIGHT HAIKU

the difference is

    they all broke my heart

        only you threw away the pieces

ODIUS BLACK BOX

Odious black box of
electronic voice-spurt
public garage of idling tongues
my lover was lost to me on one such
instrument of war controlled by
dirty fingers
feeling persecuted as a deranged pet in a
sunken living room
responding to inner Pavlovian commands
I mutilated the mouthpiece
shattering live plastic on the floor
tiny operators bailed out with headsets
and my lover went next door

BECAUSE I WOULD DO YOUR BIDDING

Because I would do your bidding
I slaughtered a fruit fly
for one of your smiles
yet I am not bothered by flies
to do them to death

Still blood follows lust
like flies follow us
and I will be slaughtering
though your smiles will stop

YOU WEAR THOSE MONKEY GLASSES

You wear those monkey glasses

with the coke bottle lenses

rolling up shit brown cords to the knee

I see you have hairy legs

to match your hairy armpits

you are so beautiful

it seems to me your beauty is real

and because you do not deodorize

I will never confuse you with a patch of

wild strawberries.

-Falcon Lake, Manitoba, 1980

GOD LOVES HIS MYSTERIES

God loves His mysteries

And Motek I love you

No matter that He makes it hard

Still there are always clues

For God believes in mystery, Motek,

To see if we be true

And God may keep the mystery if

Motek, He lets go of you.

Tivon, Israel, 1981

BOB DYLAN WAS MY LAST IDOL

Bob Dylan was my last idol,

approximately,

singing through all kinds of weather

you know idols are so good for making you feel like

you got a friend

when you don't

Bob was a helluva sacreligious atheist

before he found Jesus

probably in Albequerque

in the back of a Cadillac

or in an empty roadside Hilton

far away from Hibbing

where it all began

Now every time I hear a gospel plow

reverberating like David's harp

stuck inside a Jewish nose

it makes me hate growing old

they all panic at thirty

and I just worry I could scandalize

my youth

I HAVE KNOWN YOU THESE THREE LIVES

I have known you these three lives

and have watched you silently spending

my last emotional dollars

in some vain attempt at keeping yourself

young and satisfied

like a virgin in a snapshot

or a tourist in the shade

always self sufficient

like the God whom you disbelieved

you designed your own star

even adding several rings

and now that your time has finally come

am I to be surprised by your absence?

DON'T SETTLE

Don't settle

not for buses or hostages

north winds or no names

demand shower heads in slum baths

drink not from the bottle

but from the glass

let warm food be hot

throw back the cat fish

take off your rubber

reject electronic tranquilizers

and lovers who just want to be friends

satisfied like vice-presidents

or dead tax payers

waiting for a refund.

New Year's Eve
Toronto, 1980

THE TROUBLE WITH THIS LOVE IS

The trouble with this love is
I am not breathing deeply
it used to smell good
like a forest after a rainfall
like a childhood memory
burst free

I once was a blind man
who inhaled my love in darkness
if she was bleeding
like a shark I could find her
if she was bleeding one drop

It is true there is a fire here
I can see someone burning
it could be the smoke
it could be the cold
I just don't smell anything

THE METHOD OF POLITENESS IS TO KEEP MOVING

I feel like a prisoner in an egg shell

if I juggled china on a stick

had herpes on the lips

or but remotely resembled the last case of

smallpox

I could understand your dodging me

like a military draft

or a country radar trap

but I don't investigate new immigrants

I never once peed in the sink

it is true I hung up after three rings

when your mother said hello

but that's because she always says it through her nose

and besides

I could have breathed

THEY ARE GOING TO CALL ME TO THE BAR

They are going to call me to the bar

In 1984

what kind of criminals shall I defend

bald heads

with bullion hidden in broom closet banks

young boys

with stilletos and scars

smugglers

knuckle dusters

perverts with flashlight eyes

flickering like home movies of

inmates in Disneyland

Soon they will come

down from the castles with a

dime in their hands my

axe men

ready to do business

in a world of mens rea

when I am called to the bar

Guilty, with a mind

Kingston, Ontario, 1983

EINSTEIN'S BRAIN

I may never understand your achievements in relativity
but I shall always be inspired by your failure in high school
with teachers well loved like terrorists
it is no wonder the compass felt warm in your hand

    like a sparrow gathered to its nest

        or a Jew fiddling in Germany
while the synagogues burned.

Outside in the courtyard
they trampled the special theories

    like young plants under jackboots

        like holy letters under prayer shawls

            like hot tears under smoldering stars
showering in Spinoza's backyard
where another tree of knowledge
is robbed of its fruit.

A scientist dreams of Heaven
and wakes to Hiroshima
invariably a cage will find a bird
and somewhere in Wichita

they study Einstein's brain

    floating in a bell jar

        like a wanton in consommé

though he vanished long ago

for a meeting of the universal mind

traveling faster than madness

through crowds.

WHY DO WE WANT TO KNOW ALL

Why do we want to know all
about the things that hurt us
is love responsible for the inner trappings that bind us
like six year olds
ambushed in dentists' chairs

who are the mad tooth slayers
and why do we want to know all
about these things
these things that hurt us
the intentional scars
leaving cavities in our chests
the size of lonely molars.

Still we remain here
mute as monkeys in space suits
standing blameless as witches on blistering coals
straining skyward
feeling no pain
while receiving the drill
and paying the installment plan of decay.

I WAS WARNED ABOUT THE BEGGARS

I was warned about the beggars

so I did not stop to count them

and when the young widow by the Nile

said

    please

showing me the baby at her

    suckless breast

I kept walking

I was warned

I could not feed them all

so I did not stop to count them

so many beggars

and a mother and her child.

-Cairo, 1981

THEY TOLD STORIES ABOUT YOU

-(for Gordon (Gavriel) Templeman, A"H)

They told stories about you

    say you followed the gold rush

        made love to some of the finest women

with street names like Selkirk, Osborne, Aberdeen

the family did not know what to make of you

who ever heard of a Jewish prospector

    from Winnipeg

        dipping his pans into rivers and streams

you could have had gaberdine

    but a man could price his dreams

        behind the counter

you would never part with yours

come Spring it was another passage

    aboard the Alaska Lady Luck

        a gold locket you sent your cousin Rachel

she always cheered for you

when you died that summer

    a free man in rapids

no one was surprised

but Rachel

who stopped going to films
        on Saturday afternoons

when I was still small
I remember her hands
        drawing me closer
                inhaling my smell
holding me still with her fingers like straws
inhaling

these days I am riding a wave
        falling out of bed with women
                whose names all sound the same
and I hear that my birth place
is full of physicians
that I have been branded a fake

well I am not going back
        to easy living and incest
                to mind someone's store
I am coming to find you
tell me you found gold
when you drowned on my birthday
and left me your name

SECOND LETTER TO COLUMBUS
FROM WEST HAWK LAKE

They are tearing down the Temples

burning books upon the street

"Could be a meltdown on the horizon,"

says the late night weatherman

"Even the birds are taking cover."

Man, if this place was not flat to begin with

it sure is changing in a hurry

just feel the lining of my wallet

or try wearing one of those dog face gas masks

there is no passage to the Orient

through this ocean of cement

there is no tea and spice buried in my backyard

so why did somebody have to go and have a

miscarriage at McDonald's?

why am I getting searched three times each morning

on my way to work

and made to lug lead statues

through the market place

on my coffee break

while the sky leaks?

THIS NORTHERN WOMAN THAT I LOVE

This northern woman that I love
    wears my heart in a leather glove
When I complain it is hot as hell
    she says that glove it fits her well

A Spanish dancer dressed in lace
    caught my eye and took her place
We wined and dined till we were full
    then I charged her like a raging bull

Now the only kitten whom I made
    withdraws her claws and acts afraid
I ask her why she sleeps alone
    she says I threw the dog a bone

Why this Russian doll I bought for free
    means nothing more than history
Like a ghost out of the past
    she comes to me like last year's fast

It occurs to me it is getting late
    to cultivate the perfect mate
Undeterred I keep my cool
    True love I know comes to a fool

STILL GOT MY HEALTH

Can't afford money
not even one cent
don't have a bed
I sleep on cement
don't got a friend
in the government
but I still got my health
it's not yet spent
I still got my health
though some others have went

    don't buy sugar
    don't like cream
    never had good love
    just in between
    don't pour dirt
    into people's washing machines
    but I still got my health
    on account of my genes
    I still got my health
    though the water's not clean

I still got my health

It's a wonderful thing

to wake up every morning

roll over and sing

don't need a castle

to feel like a king

I still got my health

like a bird got a wing

still got my health

though I be hanging by a string

-Toronto, 1985

I LEFT MY WINDOW OPEN

I left my window open
on a hot summer's night
and the call of a woman
stirred my soul from deepest sleep
it was a very gentle sound
like the moaning of a deer
struck by moonlight on the highway
it was a very plaintive sound
of a vaporizing genie
who I could see now
in her silk Arabian dress
struggling in the curtains
of the balcony above
it was the very secret sound
the sound of a woman
slowly making her love
it was a very holy sound
the sound of genies
and deers
on a hot summer's night

- Ronnie's room, Kensington Market, Toronto, 1979

VALEDICTION FORBIDDING CANOEING

The last time that I saw her
    she was living with a man
Her soul beside a blue canoe
    stuck upon dry land

She never loved canoeing
    the thought that she could tip
Yet she let me climb aboard
    Before they finally split

Oh the muddy shores of love
    When you paddle into shame
Oh the muddy shores of love
    When you Portage over Main

-Winnipeg, 1980

THE JEWS' CHANT

In Russian forests Cossacks chase me
In Europe's soil Nazis slay me
In America my own betray me
In every land the stranger hates me

I've been spurned and foiled
    rubbled and raked,
Burned and boiled
    bubbled and baked
Lit in rings, shot in squares
    tied by chains and thrown down stairs

I have given both my heart and mind
    to hostile worlds still unkind
Though by the law I have lived these years
    sad eyed angels weep my tears

Holy One! I believe the time
    has come for me to make the climb
Two thousand years among the nations
    Redeem us from our desperation!

In Russian forests Cossacks chase me

In Europe's soil Nazis slay me

In America my own betray me

In every land the stranger hates me.

-San Francisco, 1973

THE PASSOVER CHANT

God pass over in a pillar of fire
God pass over in a pillar of cloud

Moses raise your staff on high
Moses lead us through the night

Lord I feel the plagues are falling
Lord I feel the plagues are near

Pharoah! Bosses! Masters beware!
Ten plagues you will breathe inside the air!

Pharoahs! Bosses! Masters of might!
The slaves are marching out tonight!

Elijah rap upon my walls
Sound the horn that no one stalls

God pass over every door
No more bondage ever more!

- San Francisco, 1973

M.

(1955-1970)

Neath the naked glow of hissing lights
    that steam into revolving night
We fled to forest fields
    limbs waving madly
Dancing like mad orphaned fools
    we slapped and clapped the backs
That Oh so proudly carried us
    as we were flung upon wet grass
You drank a molten brew of stars
    that melted on your tongue
Meteor falls of fire balls
    escaped in smoke upon your song
And while the rain like metal spears
    aimed at our forward path
Your eyes, like moons, so soft and warm
    Looked up but were ashamed to ask
David and boy Jonathan
    star shields shining at our sides
We climbed into the night
Wild figures flashing
My heart was pounding in my chest
    when thunder cracked the sky

I thought our arms were lost
 and then I caught you!
With my throat, eyes, ears and nose
 transferred to my mouth
I drew my senses through you
 and tasted laughter
"Your brother love is sweeter love
 than any of the women,"
King David spoke and tore his coat
 but Jonathan could not hear him
Like the cloud that smothers the stubborn sun
 the nightmare seized the dream
The one alive, in love with life
 now is nowhere to be seen
I knocked my knees and sunk my head
 I cursed at first then swallowed
Motionless, I swung my fist
 At the ghost who stole a child
Whose orders these? Whose battle plans?
 were they yours or the Angel's of death?
Why you held a sword, a fiery sword
 and he held only breath
Why he held only breath.

-San Francisco, 1973

WESTERN HAIKU

Sex

    and more sex until death

        the sad animal sleeps

ALLIE

Allie
in her silk pyjamas
eyes green as mars
parading down the highway
stepping here
    stopping there
always in between
cocoons of silence

mist gathering at her heels
red fire hatching under her shirt
tightening a cowboy belt
made from pearls and yellow beads
Allie rests her hips

she peaks past midnight
when the traffic is heavy
and the gas light dims
she turns up the aisle
and cruises

all men have loved a waitress

hand maiden of the western world

sea horse of rivulet cafes

bending knees

attracting tips

Allie is an Apache pastiche

leather bound for common men

swirling by tables

while wooden legs sigh

she takes note of my tea leaves

and wonders

will that be all?

THE MAN WITH THE PHOTOGRAPHS WOULD NOT LIE

the man with the photographs would not lie

he said he saw you squirming in the tomb

and the girl with the Spanish fly under one arm

wasn't joking when she raised the other

in a stiff salute."

"You know somethin, baby?"

say them both.

"You're not perfect yet

but you just may

the prettiest angel

we ever seen without wings".

so pleased to meet ya, honey

it was a crazy kind of vision

somewhere's near Medicine Hat

I was desperate on the back roads

and my foot fell asleep on the gas

you know we breezed and then

we coasted some

like a pair of hooded backseat lovers

we paid all kinds of fines for this exposure

and had to charge them back to your legal name.

now but distant remains of sunset movies fading fast

and these, your billboards made from ice paper and nails

scraping snowflakes, hiding clues,

on this bloodhound search for wives and fools.

your religion does not interest me

neither does your pain

a train is all I am after

a train with a thousand whistles

a train with a thousand stops

a train where no man gets on

a train where no man gets off

a train of love

and a train with want adds

filled by flesh and chilled by blood.

that's what I want

that's who I am

with no baggage to weigh down

once crippled gypsy moth in heat

with no lips to kiss and seal

seven beggars fortunes in the night

with hearts missing

with souls singing

with dreams bleeding

with truth awakening past the dawn

and the moon still jealous of your guiding light.

I SAW THE GLAZED EYES OF THE HOSTAGE

I saw the glazed eyes of the hostage
I was in my bathrobe in the living room
he was in Iran on TV
A marine
    he was handsome.

Young American
probably never been outside Pueblo, Colorado
before getting stationed over there in Tehran
looking nervously at newsmen
    the weird students around him
answering "yes sir" or "no sir"
    "the President is
    my commander sir"
we loved him for not breaking.

And then broke the networks
with pimple lotion
    and food frozen
    and life tasting beer
while the hostage on hold
apologized to students
who rolled over and cheered.

And I felt like a hostage

though bound by other Ayatollahs

    similar Shahs

I could see no release

for I was meaningless

    and helpless

        and like him

I was broke.

-Eugene, Oregon, 1979

WHY DOES ARAFAT WEAR SUNGLASSES

Why does Arafat wear sunglasses
Why do Klansmen hide in hoods
Know me by my enemies
Who would perish in the daylight

Why did Eichman build the showers
Why were death camps kept a secret
Know me by my enemies
Who would murder little children

Why do the new sons speak in code
Death to Zionists not to Jews
Know me by my enemies
Who wait for me with nets

Why won't the Kremlin let us go
Why won't the Pope ever get upset
Know me by my enemies
More consistent than my friends

Why does Israel stand alone
Why do nations come and go
Know me by my enemies

GOT TO HAVE THE WILL (TO SURVIVE)

When your baby's blood is boiling
    and in the morning starts a freezing
When her kisses says she's yours
    and her suitcase says she's leaving
You can holler at the moon
    you can stand upon your head
You can try and stop her train
    or you can let it go instead
When you know that love can kill
    and still the help just don't arrive
That's when you got to have the will
        (to survive).

When you open up the mail
    and there's bills you got to pay
When you feel the jar is empty
    and today's a rainy day
When the forecast says sun showers
    and it turns into a flood
When the earth you used to stand on
    crumbles into mud
When you know that love can kill
    and still the help just don't arrive

That's when you got to have the will
            (to survive)

When the doctor wants to see you
        and asks you to sit and not to stand
When he orders you to smoke
        and take up a stronger brand
You know you should have told that woman
        she was damage to your health
But instead you chose to see her
        now you've gone and hurt yourself
When you know that love can kill
        and still the help just don't arrive
That's when you got to have the will
            (to survive)

Now it's somewhere's in between
        the cradle and the grave
You once were independent
        you're now a useless slave
The clock upon the wall
        says you're running out of time
Your baby's gone for good
        and you're left without a dime
When you know that love can kill
        and still the help just don't arrive
That's when you got to have the will
            (to survive)

44

IT RAINED ALL NIGHT

It rained all night
that night
when I wept neath your window
and searched past your door
it rained waterfalls of pity
and gushed buckets of love

It's a wonder you came out at all
that night
bathing in the soft white light of the moon
stepping in shadows, speaking of dreams
you were so easy
and I was so sure of the truth

The keepers of the forest were surely watching
that night
when holding your hand
I led you by brooks
and covered your back
with fall's grape blooded leaves
I wanted to be wed at midnight
that night
wed by the birds whose wings

were like prayer

blessed by the high priests

who stood guard at the gates

For I know I stood naked on

that night

like no other

diving from caves

into emerald pools

blowing your hair from my eyes

Receiving your gifts through

that night

when the wind fell

beating our backs

to the drum and the rain

healing your flesh

pressing your lips

I loved you forever

that night

never dawning

I slept with your secrets

and fought with your fate

I pretended your enemy was dead

When you came to me

that night

you came without warning

and sealing my forehead

you told me my name

why you spoke it but once on

that night

never ending

why you left me for dead on

that night

when you left

THE LAST TIME WE MADE LOVE

The last time we made love

down in the mine shaft

a wailing jackhammer accompanied the motions

of a runaway avalanche

with serpentine jazz raining pebbles and gold

from the old walls

it felt good to be gathered there to rock

(like loadstone to magnet)

it felt fine punching overtime

in the centre of the earth.

"There are no mistakes in the universe"

that's what you whispered in my ear

and I heard you neath my hard hat

with the low beams flickering

like loose static on the back of cat tails.

There are no mistakes

only accidents that are planned

and people who are mistaken

for their love.

SEALED IN A RAINCOAT

sealed in a raincoat
she arrive at the doorstep
it is late afternoon
I listen to jah music

she undress by the window
she tease all the rain
she Moabite priestess
preparing to do love

tigress mane tumble down
black locks like a raven
outside the rain swells
in the window a mirror

like slaves who are bathing
colours washing down river
singing songs of redemption
feeling breath warm touch the arm

IF I AUDITION FOR YOUR ARMY, MAJOR

If I audition for your army, major
    with slingshots in my hands
Do not order me to serve you
    with my head beneath the sand
Do not order me to serve you
    by any law of man's
I perform not for a medal
    When I follow His commands.

And when I occupy your table, surgeon
    let us both be wearing masks
That neither may reveal
    the nature of his tasks
That neither may reveal
    that neither one should ask
Why must we share this moment
    we know to be the last.

THE LAST POEM IN THE WORLD

The last poem in the world
was the Ode to Butterflies
butterflies for catching in hands butterflies
butterflies for setting free

The Ode to Butterflies
by an anonymous poet of six years

diamond-speckled humpbacks   born in Poland
barb-wire red wings   deported to Auschwitz
melt in the sunlight   swept up a smokestack

become as tears.

It was the winter of 1942
when the last poem in the world
was first published.

STRANGE FIRE

LOVE RIDES IN ON A HORSE

love rides in on a horse

and leaves with a limp

I fall by the roadside

struck

like the terrible child

who let the secret out

growing bolder I rise

and turn the lights on

forgetting all the while

love only survives

in the mutual dark

GETTING CLOSE TO YOU

getting close to you
is like feeding sugar to a deer
there is an art to hesitation
to all things willed

grabbing hold of your heart
is to catch a snowflake on the tongue
there is a method to tenderness
however unskilled

lying beside you
is to breathe without breath
there is a secret to love
be still, be still

OUT OF LOVE

Out of love
I seldom write these
things called poems but for you I will try to poet
and wrap tiny word gems
around your white ankles
I will hold up a train or a stage coach
of thought
(for even if you don't love me and me only
the way you love everybody else is somehow inspiring)

but say do you love me
pretty blonde girl with
swimmable blue eyes
marble eyes, sea-shell eyes,
I know you love the others
I know about you and them
plainclothes lovers
staking you out
(why you could even make love to your enemies
the way that you smile)

but now that it's time to take our leave
down the boardwalk
me in my walking pneumonia
and you who spoke to me once of love
while I tried to concentrate on the shape
and colour of your unitarian nose in winter
replaying your telephone voice through the
disappearing funnel of my mind
losing you
but wanting you close like
the rain in my fist like
the last dance or
the hope that remains in
a pawnshop guitar

MY HEART SINKING FASTER

my heart sinking faster
    than the stone I send skimming
        six times over the grey Canadian lake

SHE SAID I INSPIRED A LITTLE TENDERNESS

She said I inspired a little tenderness

in her and wished to leave the party

to find somewhere

anywhere

to make love

her and me

that's what she said to me

nobody ever said it quite like

that to me

or did it

for that matter

quite so tenderly

her making love to me

her making love to me

her making love to me

THE DANCE FLOOR FILLED WITH WATER

The dance floor fills with water

I see you swimming from the shore

through the liquid air I feel your

ring of waves

swirling

the steam rising beyond the marble arches

your fingers like fish

darting through cupped hands

is it true you hear the secret pitch that

guides the dolphin through the depths

tell me who it is that moves you

in the middle of the night

your moonlit legs tredding high above the jagged reef

keep on dancing

in fields, by truck stops,

in rain filled endless highways

keep moving

on hot coals, over broken glass

in between bridges

under torch-lit enemy skies

heal them

splash them

with two parts rhythm

and spice

ease their stone feet out

from where they are stuck on dry land

like riverbank statues

stone trees weeping

while you step in and out of

the endless transmission

like a pagan let loose

in a temple of believers

FAMILY GATHERING

family gathering

deep inside yet another downtown oasis

we keep wandering

red sea pedestrians

mingling like the mismatched federal buildings

post offices and other assorted watchtower outposts

of the vast American desert

checking ourselves into iron tent hotels

paying urban respects on

the back of blank guest room checks

checking ourselves out

while one generation grows

and the other disappears

only to become anointed overnight

hail the newborn messengers

carrying genetic greetings from afar

a lost son's brow raised

gently over familiar eyes

of the future bride

while blind orphans dance

holding hands across the jeweled ballrooms

of the American sheikhdoms

stretching shoulder to shoulder

cheek to cheek

spreading a human hora of flesh beyond

the age of uncertainty

uniting the spheres of all heaven and earth

roping loose souls

pulling them down

into the lobby like temple of

this traveling hotel

this Hebrew Hilton

with its portable ark hidden

somewhere on the balcony of the mezzanine

and now that we must take our leave

with chests unpacked and

historical baggage too secure

for the fate which we tempt

recalling the first reservation in

the Babylon Inn

here in the leap year of our exile

we will pick up the pieces

of shattered glass

left trampled underfoot

and drink "L'Chaim" – to life

we shall pick up the pieces

and put them in our pockets

with our room keys

and our road maps

till the next celebration

till the next gathering

in the suburbs

or the shtetl

to wherever we are traveling

to be family once more.

ANGELS DON'T LEAVE FOOTPRINTS

Angels don't leave footprints
They don't leave calling cards
And neither do you leave past lives
When you enter the door to my heart

Blind men don't need signposts
When they cross into the alley
And venture into chaos
Stopping traffic in the dark

Kindness can be cruel
When you lie to tell the truth
When you try to feed a shark
And ask it not to bite you

Fools never know what hit them
When they wake up in the playhouse
And the only light says Exit
And the crowd has all gone home

WON'T YOU SEND ME SOMEBODY TO LOVE (OH LORD)

I don't need any money
    I pay the bills on time
I feel like a racehorse
    hitting my prime
There is nothing I lack
    that you did not think of
Oh won't you send me somebody
    somebody to love

I don't need a date
    a night on the town
I'm not looking for thrills
    they just bring me down
I'd rather stay home
    if push comes to shove
Oh won't you send me somebody
    somebody to love

I don't have any worries
    I'm a self made man
I climb many mountains
    just because I can
I fly my own plane
    in the skies high above

Oh won't you send me somebody
    somebody to love

Chorus: Somebody not taken
        Who won't use or betray
        Somebody who's real
        For that somebody I pray

        Let her be somebody good,
        Somebody kind
        I've looked the world over
        But she's so hard to find

I know that she is out there
    I have met her before
She's that voice in my ear
    from a distant shore

She appears in my dream
    in the stars high above
Oh won't you send me somebody
    somebody to love

My name it is written
    between her dark eyes
The truth will triumph
    over all of the lies

I know that she fits
  my hand like a glove
Oh won't you send me somebody
  somebody to love

I have no desire
  I eat what I kill
Spare me adventure
  I don't seek any thrill

But I don't want the raven
  I will wait for the dove
Oh won't you send me somebody
  somebody to love

Chorus: Somebody not taken
            Who won't use or betray
            Somebody who's real
            For that somebody I pray

            Let her be somebody good,
            Somebody kind
            I've looked the world over
            But she's so hard to find

SHALL WE WALK NO MORE

Shall we walk no more

on the jagged stones of Barcelona

stepping in and out of shadows

lit by pails of moonlight

stay with me, Oriana

guide me through the golden fog before the dawn

please don't let go of the

last Spanish Jew to return from exile

since 1492

Hold me, Oriana, through the modern Inquisition

touch me with your Catalan tongue

heart fluttering like a dove under cover

let's walk this night together, Oriana,

you in your knee high boots of

Spanish leather

me with Jacob's ladder

tied to my back

and my pockets full of holy Hebrew letters on fire

as Christopher Columbus

looks down from his sailing ship in the sky

and love itself is the wind

-Barcelona, 2004

WHERE DO BIRDS GO WHEN THEY DIE?

Where do birds go when they die
I have yet to see one fall from the sky
and fish not swallowed alive
do they float to the top when their time arrives
or swim to the edge of the ocean tide
where do fish go when they die?

where does the time go
when it is all used up
like tiny drops that cling to
the bottom of a paper cup
where does the time go?

and dreams
that shatter the breaking dawn
like naked truth
or forgotten yawn
where do dreams go
when they are gone?

DOWN ON MYSELF

Down on myself

dry for a moonless month

floating through an endless night

like a wayward drone

gushing forth like a torrent

in the wilderness

bursting like a flower

through a crack in a Precambrian rock

this poem for you

WHERE IN THE WORLD

Oh, where in the world are you
I search in crowded streets
where shadows empty upon the pavement
like loose change from so many pickpocket thieves
And who are you stalking
in this abrupt history
of vacant love, mutilated hearts
on display here in the museum of unborn embryos
of tiny, unanswered prayers laid bare

Oh, why are you absent from the master painting
When will you show your naked self
and disrupt the humiliation of
illusion chasing dream girls
with assorted untouchables in tow

Oh, where in the world are your
venerable ancestors, my dear,
and why have they not begotten you
to me before the end of time
comes crashing to a halt

Oh, where in the world are you
I smell your blood
taste your kisses between the
summer sickles
I see your hidden face hanging
from the movie screen
like an invitation to war

Oh, where in the world are you
and why do you tarry
dragging an iron glove
that shields you
from the bloody centuries of disbelief
I long to hold your destiny
between the lips of my vanishing song
I long to catch your breath
to undress your thoughts
with my unsatisfied mind

STUNG BY YOUR BETRAYAL

Stung by your betrayal

like a blind-sided pedestrian

I will never walk the same again.

I will cover my back

from love's crack assassins.

I will fashion an armour laden breastplate

over my open heart

that even the sharpest of words

may not pierce.

Like an outlaw on the run

I vow never to sleep in the same bed twice.

No one can hurt you

like the one who loves you

and no one can love without pain.

For only love can be both the cure and the disease

and that is no remedy at all.

THE BIRDS OF THE WESTERN WALL

The birds of the Western Wall
circle high above the courtyard
sunlight retracting like a red ball of string
rolling up the purple hills
ribbons of darkness descending
while two legged worshippers below
dressed in black with white fringes
like feathers
swaying back and forth
hot prayers on mystical lips
soaring above clouds
rising like steam from open hearts

The birds of the Western Wall
dart inside secret clefts in the rock
black letters of fire and ice
swirling in the wind
like forgotten sparks in the night
harnessing the energy of souls
driven by a whirlpool of love and prayer
the still small voice calling them home

The birds of the Western Wall

melt into stone

the crimson sunset strikes

and the Sabbath Queen appears

casting a majestic shadow

somewhere so precisely

between Heaven and earth

-Jerusalem, 2000

SOMEWHERE OVER THE OCEAN

Somewhere over the ocean
where the sun and moon collide
we started a conversation
at least to talk to you I tried

You wore a simple smile
I wore a surgeon's mask
You revealed to me your name
I only had to ask

Shani is a ribbon of scarlet
Shani is a crimson thread
Shani is a pool in the wilderness
Where the tears of the sinners bled

What Heavenly smile did you inherit
Shani of the open skies
the glory of the Temple
still sparkles in your eyes

for Shani is a ribbon of scarlet
Shani is a crimson thread
Shani is a desert sandstorm
fading into red

-LY Flight 32 somewhere over the Atlantic, 2003

THERE IS A LAND

There is a land
dressed in white
with rivers and streams
that flow fiercely
from jagged mountain tops
with sheaves of wheat
golden sunflowers
that arch proudly
before infinite skies

There is a land
where the sun sets like honey
on the oceanside
and the falcon and the eagle
glide side by side in
perfect autumn jetstreams
while spoonfulls of waterdrops
glisten on a lone wooden paddle
brushing mystic ripples
to distant shores

There is a land
where the tall trees whisper in the wind
and the children grow
with fairness in their hearts
like diamonds in the snow
born of courage
torn from elements
unafraid to stand
even on one leg
willing to walk the distance alone

daring to risk all
if the cause be but just

There is a land of fire and ice
and northern lights
of 49 parallels of hope
and ribbons of steel
crossed by magical trains

There is a land
that fears not to speak its mind
in a world gone mad
determined like the rock in its shield
to be true

JONATHON POLLARD MUST DIE

Jonathon Pollard must die
my American cousin lied
when he says he came to his side
he would rather put a bullet in his head
and make sure he was dead

So he was betrayed in the end
when they refused to defend
his stealing from a friend
secrets that saved lives,
albeit only Jewish ones.

Hey my American cousin
like Jack Ruby before
let no man doubt you are more
American than Jew
more red white and blue
more apple pie than knish
no debate about this

Let no President fear
that what we have here
is one of our own
who acted alone
for it is well known
there is no Jewish home
like the goldena medina

Let him rot inside
says my cousin with pride
I wish he had died

for he did this to me
he's no brother of mine
let him do all the time.

And so he dies a slow death
thirty years no protest
no Pardon request
too embarrassed to ask why
who likes a Jewish spy
it would be better he die
and leave well alone.

LOVE IS SOMETHING YOU DO

Love is something you do

she said

upon doing it for the first time

coming when I never called her

women are like cats

they never come when you call

and what does this old man know from

cats and women

all I know is dogs

and how to whistle like a fool

THERE IS NO ONE MORE BEAUTIFUL

There is no one more beautiful
than the bride at her wedding
though my eyes went wandering
like a last minute groom
like a groom with no last name
or fixed address
to offer his beloved

we must have looked suspect
you like a minstrel, gazelle or
black jack of hearts
missing from the dealer's hand
me in my rented tuxedo and stolen shoes
seeming a convict on the run

fortunately there are no police at weddings
and perhaps I will meet your husband some other time
for tomorrow when he greets you
and the children surprise you in bed
I will be somewhere in Scotland
traveling the train of our conversation
looking out through the mist in your eyes
trying to remember what exactly was left unsaid
and how will I ever see you again

MUMBAI MOON

(for Anat)

Mumbai moon, Mumbai moon,
washing through scented streets
children laughing in the gutter
crimson, orange, saffron robes
three wheel taxis spin and sputter

Mumbai moon, Mumbai moon,
incense, smoke, blind and lame
barefoot shadows moving
glowing embers of temple shrines
sound of peddlars snoozing

Mumbai moon, Mumbai moon
spotlight shining like a river
spice like smell perfuming
dancing elephants flutes and horns
servants in white turbans looming

Mumbai moon, Mumbai moon
cobra headboard above the bed
a curiosity for the dead
miracle potions, lover lotions
Signs abound all confusing

Mumbai moon, Mumbai moon,
a lone actor on the stage
all the words have left the page
a thousand eyes hypnotized
so enchanting, so amusing

-Mumbai, 2015

FISTFUL OF DOLLARS

You got a fistful of dollars
A treasure chest of gold
Your well is filled with oil
And all of its been sold
You have an army of assassins
And missiles put on hold
Servants all around you
And statues in your mold
But none of that will matter
As the truth will yet be told
And I'll be there to greet you
When you come in from the cold
And I'll be there to meet you
When the Judgment Day unfolds

You live by the sword
Your hand on every man
Attacking from the rear
The only way you can
You educate your children
To die on your command
For a world that you desire
Where every freedom's banned
But none of that will matter
As the truth will yet be told
And I'll be there to greet you
When you come in from the cold
And I'll be there to meet you
When the Judgment Day unfolds

You ruin and destroy
Everything you touch
Then cry that you're the victim
That no one likes you much
You lie and then you lie some more
And say it's done as such
Taking shelter in a schoolyard
And leaning on a crutch
But none of that will matter
As the truth will yet be told
And I'll be there to greet you
When you come in from the cold
And I'll be there to meet you
When the Judgment Day unfolds

www.ingramcontent.com/pod-product-compliance
Lightning Source LLC
LaVergne TN
LVHW091205080426
835509LV00006B/834